Our Holidays

Celebrate Valentine's Day

Amy Hayes

Cavendish Square

New York

Published in 2015 by Cavendish Square Publishing, LLC
243 5th Avenue, Suite 136, New York, NY 10016

Copyright © 2015 by Cavendish Square Publishing, LLC

First Edition

Website: cavendishsq.com

This publication represents the opinions and views of the author based on his or her personal experience, knowledge, and research. The information in this book serves as a general guide only. The author and publisher have used their best efforts in preparing this book and disclaim liability rising directly or indirectly from the use and application of this book.

CPSIA Compliance Information: Batch #WW15CSQ

All websites were available and accurate when this book was sent to press.

Library of Congress Cataloging-in-Publication Data

Hayes, Amy.
Celebrate Valentine's Day / Amy Hayes.
pages cm. — (Our holidays)
Includes index.
ISBN 978-1-50260-236-7 (hardcover) ISBN 978-1-50260-243-5 (paperback) ISBN 978-1-50260-241-1 (ebook)
1. Valentine's Day—Juvenile literature. I. Title.

GT4925H39 2015
394.2618—dc23

2014032649

Senior Copy Editor: Wendy A. Reynolds
Art Director: Jeffrey Talbot
Designer: Joseph Macri
Senior Production Manager: Jennifer Ryder-Talbot
Production Editor: David McNamara
Photo Researcher: J8 Media

The photographs in this book are used by permission and through the courtesy of:
Cover photo by Digital Vision/Getty Images; KidStock/Blend Images/Getty Images, 5; Benjamin A. Peterson/Mother Image/mother image/Fuse/Thinkstock, 7; Joseph Macri for Cavendish Square, 9; ©iStockphoto.com/sdominick, 11; David Johnston/Photolibrary/Getty Images, 13; ©iStockphoto.com/kirin_photo, 15; rockvillepikephoto/iStock/Thinkstock, 17; Jamie Grill/Getty Images, 19; nkbimages/E+/Getty Images, 21.

Printed in the United States of America

Contents

Today is Valentine's Day!

4

5

Valentine's Day is a day to **celebrate** love.

We tell people we love that we care about them.

7

Valentine's Day happens every year on February 14.

Today is February 14.

FEBRUARY

Sunday	Monday	Tuesday	Wednesday	Thursday	Friday	Saturday
1	2	3	4	5	6	7
8	9	10	11	12	13	14
15	16	17	18	19	20	21
22	23	24	25	26	27	28

9

We are going to make
valentines.

We will need supplies to make
a card.

10

11

Making valentines is fun.

Jenna and Kate make valentines together.

13

Time to give out the valentines!

Julie and Jamal give their
mom their cards.

14

On Valentine's Day we make sweet treats.

We make **cupcakes** and cookies.

16

We give treats to the people we love.

Sharing **sweets** shows that we care.

19

Valentine's Day is so much fun!

Happy Valentine's Day!

20

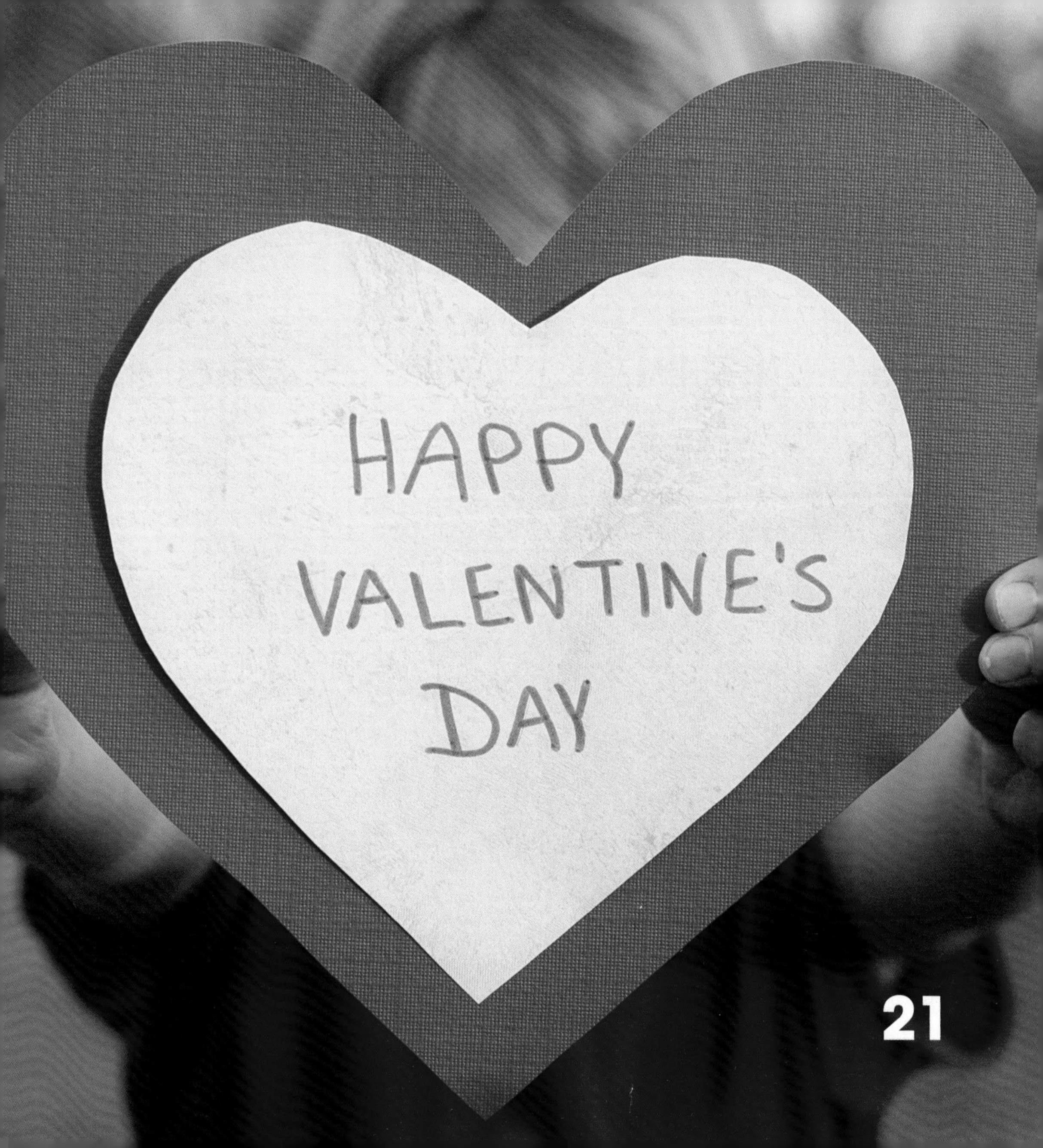
HAPPY
VALENTINE'S
DAY

New Words

celebrate (SELL-e-brate) To do something special for a holiday.

cupcakes (KUP-kakes) Very small cakes shaped like cups, usually with icing.

sweets (SWEETS) Sugary foods that are eaten as desserts or snacks.

valentines (VAL-en-tyns) Cards you give on Valentine's Day.

Index

About the Author

Amy Hayes lives in the beautiful city of Buffalo. She celebrates Valentine's Day with the people she loves.

About

Bookworms help independent readers gain reading confidence through high-frequency words, simple sentences, and strong picture/text support. Each book explores a concept that helps children relate what they read to the world they live in.